First World War
and Army of Occupation
War Diary
France, Belgium and Germany

41 DIVISION
Divisional Troops
Divisional Ammunition Column
5 May 1916 - 29 October 1917

WO95/2625/8

The Naval & Military Press Ltd
www.nmarchive.com
Published in association with The National Archives

Published by

The Naval & Military Press Ltd

Unit 10 Ridgewood Industrial Park,

Uckfield, East Sussex,

TN22 5QE England

Tel: +44 (0) 1825 749494

www.naval-military-press.com

www.nmarchive.com

This diary has been reprinted in facsimile from the original. Any imperfections are inevitably reproduced and the quality may fall short of modern type and cartographic standards.

© Crown Copyright
Images reproduced by permission of The National Archives, London, England, 2015.

Contents

Document type	Place/Title	Date From	Date To
War Diary	WO95/2625/10 41 Div Div Ammunition Column May 1916-Oct 1917		
War Diary	Aldershot	05/05/1916	05/05/1916
War Diary	Southampton	05/05/1916	05/05/1916
War Diary	Havre	06/05/1916	20/05/1916
War Diary	Caestre	21/05/1916	21/05/1916
War Diary	Borre	22/05/1916	28/05/1916
War Diary	Lefaux	31/05/1916	31/05/1916
War Diary	Borre	19/06/1916	19/06/1916
War Diary	Borre	09/06/1916	09/06/1916
War Diary	St. Sylvestre Cappel	09/06/1916	09/06/1916
War Diary	Le Veau	01/06/1916	30/06/1916
War Diary	St Sylvestre Cappel	26/07/1916	26/07/1916
War Diary	Le Veau	03/07/1916	15/07/1916
Miscellaneous	H.Q. 41st Division.	01/09/1916	01/09/1916
War Diary	Steenwerck	05/08/1916	20/08/1916
War Diary	Eecke & Bailleul	23/08/1916	24/08/1916
War Diary	L'Etoile	01/09/1916	01/09/1916
War Diary	Picquigny	02/09/1916	02/09/1916
War Diary	Dernancourt	04/09/1916	08/09/1916
War Diary	Albert	09/09/1916	15/09/1916
War Diary	Mametz	16/09/1916	09/10/1916
War Diary	Bazentin le Grand & Bernafay Wood	10/10/1916	31/10/1916
War Diary	Dernancourt	01/11/1916	01/11/1916
War Diary	Bonnay	03/11/1916	03/11/1916
War Diary	Villers-Bocage	04/11/1916	04/11/1916
War Diary	Orville	05/11/1916	05/11/1916
War Diary	Vacquerie Le Boucq	06/11/1916	06/11/1916
War Diary	Bergueneuse	09/11/1916	09/11/1916
War Diary	Ham-En-Artois	10/11/1916	10/11/1916
War Diary	Wallon Cappel	11/11/1916	11/11/1916
War Diary	Abeele	13/11/1916	13/11/1916
War Diary	H. 13 Central	21/11/1916	26/12/1916
War Diary	Zevecoten	28/12/1916	15/04/1917
War Diary	Same Place	01/05/1917	18/06/1917
War Diary	Sht. 28. S.W. M.6.b.6.8	22/06/1917	22/06/1917
War Diary	M.6.b.6.8	05/07/1917	05/07/1917
War Diary	Q. 24.a.	11/07/1917	22/07/1917
War Diary	N.4.c.4.3.	22/07/1917	01/09/1917
War Diary	R.5.a.8.6	03/09/1917	10/09/1917
War Diary	N.3.b.7.5	12/09/1917	08/10/1917
War Diary	X.7.c.8.7	14/10/1917	25/10/1917
War Diary	D. 22	29/10/1917	29/10/1917

WO95/2625/10
41 DIV
DIV AMMUNITION COLUMN
MAR 1916 – OCT 1917

Vol I May
D.A.R.
41 A.C.

Army Form C. 2118

WAR DIARY
or
INTELLIGENCE SUMMARY

(Erase heading not required.)

Instructions regarding War Diaries and Intelligence Summaries are contained in F. S. Regs, Part II. and the Staff Manual respectively. Title Pages will be prepared in manuscript.

Place	Date	Hour	Summary of Events and Information	Remarks and references to Appendices
ALDERSHOT	3.5.16	4 AM	Unit left for Port of embarkation SOUTHAMPTON in eight Troop Trains	
SOUTHAMPTON	5.5.16	12 noon	Embarked on S.S. "COURTFIELD" & ROSETTI	
HAVRE	6.5.16	9 AM	Disembarked	
—	—	3 pm	Proceeded to N°.2 Rest Camp	
—	15.5.16	9 AM	Unit was Reorganised & formed into 4 Section B Echelon 41st D.A.C. R.F.A all surplus men & Horses Equipment & Returned to Respective Departments.	
—	20.5.16	12 noon	Marched away to entrain to proceed to the front	
CAESTRE	21.5.16	6 pm	Disentrained at CAESTRE (MAP Sheet 27) & marched by Road to Billets at BORRE	
BORRE	22.5.16	9 AM	Took over the B.A.C's of the 163rd, 167th, 189th & 190th Brigades R.F.A & Reformed them into N°. 1, 2, & 3 Sections 41st D.A.C. 'A' ECHELON.	
—	25.5.16	7 AM	B. Echelon N°.4 Section proceeded by Road to LE VEAU. to assist the R.E.	
—	—	8 AM	16 G.S. Wagons were sent from 'A' Echelon to assist Batteries in Supplying Ammunition From Dump.	

A.R. [signature], Major R.F.A.
Commanding 41 D.A.C. R.F.A

41 Div Am Col
Army Form C. 2118
Add to Vol 1

WAR DIARY
or
INTELLIGENCE SUMMARY
(Erase heading not required.)

Place	Date	Hour	Summary of Events and Information	Remarks and references to Appendices
Le Veau	31/5/16	—	"B" Echelon, together with Headquarters of Divisional Ammunition Column, was formed about 6th May 1916 out of the remnants of the original D.A.C. which was disbanded on that date. As soon as the Echelon was complete with its personnel equipment it left Havre (LE HAVRE) and proceeded to Borre (BORRE). On arrival at Borre on the 20th May 1916 the following officers were posted to it:— Captain J. Bennett (J BENNETT) Lieut. G.W.F. Blythe (G.W.F. BLYTHE) 2nd Lieut. D. Vyle (D. VYLE) 2nd Lieut. J. Bending (T. BENDING) On the 29th May 1916 "B" Echelon marched out in full strength to the village of LE VEAU to take its halt in the operations then going on. The unit was still in LE VEAU on the 31st of May 1916 employed on fatigue work by the Engineers.	

J Bennett Captain RFA
O.C. "B" Echelon D.A.C.

Army Form C. 2118

WAR DIARY
or
INTELLIGENCE SUMMARY
(Erase heading not required.)

Place	Date	Hour	Summary of Events and Information	Remarks and references to Appendices
BORRE	19.6.16	7 AM	Change Billets marched by Road to EECKE — SAINT SYLVESTRE CAPPEL Gr (Sheet 27)	
"	—	—	Between the 1st & 9th June 10 N.cos & all Gunners were sent up to Batteries to assist in making entrenchments. It was whilst on this fatigue that the 1st Casualty in the Unit occurred, No. 1302. Gunner G.E. Wand No. 3 Section was shot in the Back & died from wounds & was interred in BAILLEUL CEMETERY. (Sheet 28). Gnr.	
ST. SYLVESTRE CAPPEL	9.6.16	8 AM		

J.R. Stamm C. Major R.A.
Commanding 41 S.S. R.G.A.

WAR DIARY
INTELLIGENCE SUMMARY

Army Form C. 2118

(Erase heading not required.)

Place	Date	Hour	Summary of Events and Information	Remarks and references to Appendices
LE VEAU	1/6/16 to 30/6/16		"B" Echelon remained at LE VEAU during the month of June 1916 carrying on fatigues for the Engineers. There have been no casualties and no change in nominal roll of officers. The unit is still at LE VEAU	

June 30th 1916

J Bennet
Captain
6ig "B" Echelon H.D.&E.

Army Form C. 2118
July
41 Div A Col
Vol 2

WAR DIARY
or
INTELLIGENCE SUMMARY
(Erase heading not required.)

Instructions regarding War Diaries and Intelligence Summaries are contained in F.S. Regs., Part II. and the Staff Manual respectively. Title Pages will be prepared in manuscript.

Place	Date	Hour	Summary of Events and Information	Remarks and references to Appendices
ST SYLVESTRE CAPPEL	26/6	—	HQ & A Echelon moved Billets ONSTEENWERCK Sh: 36 B. 19. C. 2. 7. Wagon Line with Batteries assisting in supplying Ammunition from Dump. No. 43/18 Gunner L FALLA, attached to Y/41 T.M. Battery, wounded. (G.S. wound)	
LEVEAU	3/7/16	10 AM	B Echelon LEVEAU Sh. 36 B. 14. A. 5. 5. 19 Wagons on R.E. Fatigue near PLOEGSTEERT Sh. 28. T. 28. B. 4. 5. were shelled by enemy. Two horses killed, one wounded, no men injured.	
	15/7/16	3.15pm	While enemy aeroplanes were flying over B Echelon Camp & being engaged by our Anti-Aircraft guns the empty FUZES fell into the horse lines. Severely wounded a mule. Remainder of month was normal. R.E. Fatigues Daily.	

R. Stewart
Major R.F.A.
Commanding 41 D.A.C. R.F.A.

To:- H.Q.
41st Division

I beg to enclose herewith the "War Diary" for the Unit under my command in accordance with R.O.D.A. 276 d/-
18-7-16

1-9-16. A.R. Hunt Lt Col R.F.A.
         Comdg. 41 D.A.C., R.F.A.

WAR DIARY or INTELLIGENCE SUMMARY

Army Form C. 2118

VOL 4

4 D.A.C. R.F.A

Place	Date	Hour	Summary of Events and Information	Remarks and references to Appendices
STEENBECQ	5.8.16	12 Noon	The HQ & No 8 Sec. being out of the Divnl Comd Area were moved to near LE VEAU. Sh 36. HQ. B.14.c.1.2 & No 3 Sec B.14.c.7.4. From 5/8/16 to 19/8/16 A Echelon provided teams to Horse Lagons for carting Gravel etc for Road Making under the orders of C.E. V Corps.	
"	20.8.16	"	The whole of the DAC moved by march route to H.Q., A Bat. & 1/2 B Sec. (less B El. Wagons & teams) EECKE Sheet 27. Q.20.D.3.3. & the rest of 1/2 B. Echelon to BAILLEUL	
EECKE & BAILLEUL	23 x 24 8/16	—	The whole of the DAC. moved by Rail to ABBEVILLE Sheet 14. HQ & A Echelon worked by Road 14 miles to Billets at L'ETOILE Lens Sheet 11. & B Echelon to EPAGNE Lens Sheet 11.	
			All M Cog! & Gunners who had been on Fatigue (digging) with Batteries were returned to Sections on the 12th Aug '16	
			B Echelon had sports on 13th Aug '16	

31/8/16

[signature] Lt. Col R.F.A
Commdg 4th D.A.C. R.F.A

WAR DIARY or INTELLIGENCE SUMMARY

Army Form C. 2118

Vol 4

4th D.A.C. R.F.A.

Place	Date	Hour	Summary of Events and Information	Remarks and references to Appendices
L'ETOILE	1.9.16	6pm	HQ & H Echelon moved by Road to the area of EPAGNE or PICQUIGNY arriving at 12 m.n. B Echelon left EPAGNE at 7pm Reaching PICQUIGNY at 4 Am 2/9/16.	Sh. Amiens No 17 B.1.
PICQUIGNY	2.9.16	9pm	The whole Unit left for DERNANCOURT Sheet 62.E. 21.A.1.8. after an overnight breakfast in area of 26 Units. Reached the Bivouac at 9am 3.9.16.	
DERNANCOURT	4.9.16	—	70 men & 80 Wagons Lent to Brigade for fatigue in preparing Gun Position	
"	5.9.16	—	1 Man on fatigue Driver Toms wounded	
"	6.9.16	—	1 Man on fatigue F. Harris B. Scholes killed 2 Horses wounded. Men Horses on Return from fatigue	
"	8.9.16	—	Unit marched to Bivouac at ALBERT E.4.C.9.6. Sh. 62?	
ALBERT	9.9.16	—	50 men on Fatigue Supplying Gun Position. The whole of the Ammunition Wagons employed Supplying Ammunition day & night. 66 G.S. Wagons & Teams carrying R.E. Material to Gun Position & 53 men sent for permanent employment at "B" Ammunition Dump. Drivers NIND & DOYLE & 1 Horse Wounded.	
"	10.9.16	—	Same as 9/9/16. Dr. Keyzor wounded.	
"	14.9.16	—	Same as 9/9/16. Dr. Singleton Killed. Dr. Howard & Page wounded. 6 Horses Killed & 1 wounded	
"	15.9.16	—	HQ & H Echelon moved to MAMETZ Sheet 62.D. F.5.C.9.6. B Echelon moved to new B Dump near LE CARGAILLOT Sheet 62.D. E.18.A.57.	arrived in Bivouac 1Am 16.9.16. B Echelon
MAMETZ	16.9.16	—	Supplying Ammunition. Very Quiet, occupied. 2 Horses wounded	
"	17.9.16	—		
"	18.9.16	—	Supplying Ammunition Day & Night. Taking us up to Gun Position. Weather Wet & going very difficult for Horses. 1 Horse Killed. 1 Sgt & 6 men Shell Shock & 3 men wounded.	
"	30.9.16	—	B Echelon Carting Ammunition from OLD FRICOURT STATION to B Dump Daily. Sheet 62.D F.11.A.1.2.	

Men working exceptionally well. Horses doing well, but showing slight signs of work whilst the weather kept fair. But when the weather broke & 10 Horses had to be worked into Bivouac to "The Ammn" up to the Guns said the RHC Horses show signs of the heavy work.

30/9/16

[Signature]
Commanding 4th D.A.C. R.F.A.

Army Form C. 2118

Vols

INTELLIGENCE SUMMARY
(Erase heading not required.)

Instructions regarding War Diaries and Intelligence Summaries are contained in F.S. Regs., Part II. and the Staff Manual respectively. Title Pages will be prepared in manuscript.

41ºC DAC RFA

Place	Date	Hour	Summary of Events and Information	Remarks and references to Appendices
MARETZ.	1.10.16	—	Bomb dropped on Bivouac during night, hit no Horse Lines. 2 Horses 102 Bde. Killed whilst on fatigue.	
"	3.10.16	—	Weather very bad. Gr. Page wounded whilst attached to A/190 Bde. 1 Horse wounded. Stopped.	
"	4.10.16	—	Owing to very bad state of roads, it was impossible to relieve ammunition in wagons so had to improvise a method of carrying it on Animals with Baskets taken from Ammn Wagons. Fact Animal carries 10 Rds.	
"	5.10.16	—	Gr. Ansteme wounded whilst attacked to A/190. Gr. A. Bacon wounded whilst attacked to A/190.	
"	6.10.16	—	Gr. Anstone Died of wounds at 3F C.C.S. Gr. James wounded, 3 Horses killed & 1 wounded through one of the Horses kicking a live Fuze in a shell at night. Dr. Wagg wounded k.o.l Sec. & 2 Horses N°1 wounded.	
"	7.10.16	—	Gr. King N°3 wounded.	
"	8.10.16	—	Gnr. N°3 attacked to YM. T.M.B. died from wounds.	
"	9.10.16	—	The whole D.A.C. moved to Hqrs H.A. Echelon to Mept. ALBERT. S.15. c.4.5. & 'B' Echelon to LONGUEVAL S.17.A.5.3. 'B' Echelon assumed charge of the H.Q. B. Ammn. Dump. L. Doyle N°3 sec wounded.	
BAZENTIN LE GRAND to BERNAFAY WOOD	10.10.16	—	'B' Echelon & 'B' Dump moved to Hqrs H.A Echelon to complete Ech. near BERNAFAY WOOD Sk. ALBERT. S.25. c.o.5. The Dump was kept very busy. Waiting to supply the 12th, 21st, 29th, & 30th Divisional Artillery	
"	12.10.16	—	57 Horses received to complete Ech. Gr. Colan, r. Chargneau 'B' Ech wounded.	
"	13.10.16	—	Gr. Marvin 'B' Ech. wounded Shellshock & O'Brien 'B' Ech wounded Shellshock.	
"	15.10.16	—	'B' Echelon Bivouac shelled had to move about 300* S. only 1 Mule being wounded.	
"	21.10.16	—	Nos 1 & 2 Sec Horse Lines shelled during night. 1 Horse N°2 Sec Wounded & destroyed.	
"	22.10.16	—	Bomb dropped on 'B' Echelon Bivouac during night. No casualties.	
"	23.10.16	—	A. Echelon Bivouac shelled during afternoon. No casualties.	
"	25.10.16	—	HQ & Echelon Bivouac shelled practically all night.	
"	26.10.16	—	HQ. Echelon Bivouac shelled practically all night.	
"	31.10.16	—	D.A.C. were enough the Line being relieved by 2nd Australian DAC. marched into Bivouac DERNANCOURT AREA Sk. ALBERT. D.16. c (appx)	

31/10/16

A Hurst B Colonel
Commanding 41 DACRFA

1875 Wt. W593/826 1,000,000 4/15 J.B.C. & A. A.D.S.S./Forms/C. 2118.

WAR DIARY
or
INTELLIGENCE SUMMARY

(Erase heading not required.)

Army Form C. 2118

Vol 6

42nd D.A.C. R.F.A.

Place	Date	Hour	Summary of Events and Information	Remarks and references to Appendices
DERNANCOURT	1/11/16	—	Refilled with Gun Amm^t at DERNANCOURT Sh. 62 d E.B.6.1.6. & marched by Road to BONNAY. I.17.C. arriving at 8.30 A.M.	
BONNAY	3.11.16	—	Marched to VILLERS - BOCAGE A.A. CENTRAL.	
VILLERS-BOCAGE	4.11.16	—	Marched to ORVILLE Sh^t LENS.11. F.S. Bad BILLETS	
ORVILLE	5.11.16	—	Marched to VACQUERIE LE BOUCQ. LENS 11. C.3.	
VACQUERIE LE BOUCQ	6.11.16	—	Marched to BERGUENEUSE LENS 11. D.1. Remained here two days. Weather very inclement.	
BERGUENEUSE	9.11.16	—	Marched to HAM-EN-ARTOIS Sh^t HAZEBROUCK S. F.5.	
HAM-EN-ARTOIS	10.11.16	—	Marched to WALLON-CAPPEL Sh^t HAZEBROUCK S. F.4.	
WALLON-CAPPEL	11.11.16	—	Marched to ABEELE (PATRICIA LINES) Sh^t HAZEBROUCK S. I.3.	
ABEELE	13.11.16	—	Arrived at Destination Sh^t BELGIUM N° 28 N.W. W.Q. at H.13 CENTRAL. Adjutant took over 41st Divⁿ Ammunition Dump from 4th AUSTRALIAN D.A.C. N°1 Sec BILLETED at G.35.a.7.1. N°2 G.35.a.5.6. N°3 G.35.d.5.3. B ECHELON at Sh^t BELGIUM N° 28 S.W. M.2.a.2.1.	
H.13 CENTRAL	14.11.16	—	LEAVES Commenced. Small %.	

R. M. Hurst Lt. Col. R.F.A.
Commanding 41 D.A.C. R.F.A.

Vol 7 Army Form C. 2118

41ˢᵗ D.A.C. R.F.A

WAR DIARY
or
INTELLIGENCE SUMMARY
(Erase heading not required.)

Place	Date	Hour	Summary of Events and Information	Remarks and references to Appendices
H.13 Central	16/12/16	—	Inspection of Animals by the G.O.C. 41ˢᵗ Division.	
"	26/12/16	—	H.Q. of D.A.C. moved to new Billet at Sheet-28 N.W. H.35.c.3.6. ZEVECOTEN. Near RENING HELST.	
ZEVECOTEN	28/12/16	—	Dump at H.13 Central was handed over to 23ʳᵈ Divisional Artillery. We had to establish a new Dump in which was included the Divisional Grenade Dump at Sheet 28. S.W. M.11.a.2.5.	
			All horses up to the Gun Line have been employed in improving the Billets + Horse standings.	
			No. 3 Section struck off duty with D.A.C. + employed by G.O.C R.A. 41ˢᵗ Dⁿ in Salvage work.	
			Officers + Gunners employed in the Gun Line as hay near Gun Positions.	
			Divisional O.P. + Divisional Exchange. N.5 Central.	
			Gun Positions of RIDGE + Crest have been drained + improved.	

R. Hunt
Lt Col. RFA
31/12/16. Commanding 41 DAC RFA

WAR DIARY
or
INTELLIGENCE SUMMARY

(Erase heading not required.)

Army Form C. 2118

Vol 8

41st D.A.C. R.F.A.

Instructions regarding War Diaries and Intelligence Summaries are contained in F. S. Regs., Part II. and the Staff Manual respectively. Title Pages will be prepared in manuscript.

Place	Date	Hour	Summary of Events and Information	Remarks and references to Appendices
ZEVECOTEN	8/1/17	—	The Re-organization of the D.A.C. was carrying out. A. ECHELON consisted of 1 + 2 Sections. The establishment of these two sections were slightly increased, the deficiencies being made up from B. ECHELON, which was slightly reduced, + the original No 2 section.	
"	23/1/17	—	On this date the original No 2 Section was handed over to & became the B.A.C. of the 189th Army Troops Brigade.	
			Ammunition being drawn from Railhead & the Batteries being entirely supplied by D.A.C. All Kinter Gunners & Spare Drivers employed on Engineering work in the Gun Line.	

31/1/17

A R Hirst
Comdg 41st D.A.C. R.F.A.

Lieut
41st D.A.C. R.F.A.

Army Form C. 2118

WAR DIARY
or
INTELLIGENCE SUMMARY
(Erase heading not required.)

4/1 OC DAC RFA

Vol 9

Instructions regarding War Diaries and Intelligence Summaries are contained in F. S. Regs., Part II. and the Staff Manual respectively. Title Pages will be prepared in manuscript.

Place	Date	Hour	Summary of Events and Information	Remarks and references to Appendices
ZEVECOTEN	1/2/17 to 28/2/17	—	Supplying Divisional Ammunition Dump from Pacific Siding. Sheet 28 NW G.10.a. supplying Ammunition direct to guns. Assisting Batteries in supplying Ammunition in Front Line, assisting All available gunners working in Front line, assisting Battery + Trench Mortar Gunners in working Gun Pits + T.M. Emplacements. A large supply of Trench Mortar Ammunition supplied to Front line.	

28/2/17

E.A.J. Richmond Lt Col RFA
Commanding 4/1 DAC RFA

Army Form C. 2118

WAR DIARY
or
INTELLIGENCE SUMMARY

(Erase heading not required.)

41st D.A.C. R.F.A.

Vol 10

Place	Date	Hour	Summary of Events and Information	Remarks and references to Appendices
ZEVECOTEN	1/3/17 to 31/3/17		Practically all Gunners have been employed in the front line making O.Ps, Gun Pits &c. all the month of March '17. 21 Gunners have been trained in 18pdr & 4.5 How: drill in the front line to meet any emergency. All spare Animals withdrawn nearer to Batteries.	

Geo. Woodward Capt R.F.A.
Commanding 41 D.A.C.R.F.A.

31/3/17

Army Form C. 2118

WAR DIARY
INTELLIGENCE SUMMARY
(Erase heading not required.)

41st D.A.C. R.F.A.

No XI

Place	Date	Hour	Summary of Events and Information	Remarks and references to Appendices
ZEVECOTEN	4/4/17	—	Handed over the Ammunition Dump at Sht 28 Sn M.11.a.3.5. to 19th Divisional Artillery. Took over New Dump at Sheet 28 N.W. G.24.d. all the mont. 1 Officer & 102 other ranks have been up in the frontline taking new Gun positions etc.	
	9/4/17	—	All the Spare Horses allowed by the War Establishment were attached into the working strength.	
	1/4/17	—	Handed 37 Horses over to 187th Brigade R.A.	
	15/4/17	—	BQMS Cokeyegorn Bannon J.A. No 1 Section were accidentally wounded at the Ammn Dump whilst examining No 1 Stand Grenades. One of these Grenades was detonated on being turned, Fuzed, exploded. Gunner Ellis No 1 Sec killed whilst working in working Trench Mortar Emplacements.	

30/4/17

J.R.Hunt Lt Col RFA
Commanding 41 DAC RFA

Army Form C. 2118

WAR DIARY
INTELLIGENCE SUMMARY
(Erase heading not required.)

41st D.A.C. R.F.A.   No 1/2

Place	Date	Hour	Summary of Events and Information	Remarks and references to Appendices
SAME PLACE.	1/5/17 to 31/5/17	—	1 Officer, all Gunners & Spare drivers digging Gun Pits, Trench Water Supp Reservoirs &c.	
	1.5.17	—	No. 43421 Dr E.F. Ing wounded whilst on Front Line Fatigue	
	5.5.17	—	Transport for daily for 120 men 167th DAC.RFA up to Front Line (Gorgas).	
	6.5.17	—	No. 1 Sec had to move to a New Camp at M.6.c.6.4.4. owing to constant shelling. Capt J. Bennett, 9/c B. Echelon attached to X Corps HQ.	
	7.5.17	—	42176 Driver E.T. Day wounded. "All" Ammn carting Ammunition to New Gun Positions nightly. Also stong Trench Untending Parties	
	13.5.17	—	5 M.D. Horses, drives & G.S. wagons arrived from 41 Dt to replace L.G.S. wagons handed to Heavy M.G.C.	
	15.5.17	—	5 L.G.S. wagons with 1 M hunter in each sent to HEAVY MACHINE GUN CORPS.	
	21.5.17	—	Took over another Ammn Dump in addition at Sh F.28 N.N. G.29.c. 2Lt E. Andrews j/c.	
	23.5.17	—	Ammn issues up to Original enlistments known (Secs 19. Arty, HQ 41 DA. G.17.5.17.)	
	25.5.17	—	Leaves 4-0 amd S. A. returns weekly to D.A.C. Supply of Ammn to New Battery Positions Carts &c.	
	27.5.17	—	1 Horse No 2 Sec wounded whilst delivering Ammn.	
		—	Dr Bissex R. (37088) wounded whilst Carting O.P. material.	
	29.5.17 /30	—	A large Convoy of 55 G.S. wagons & 55 G.S. wagons detailed to deliver Heavy Trench Mortars (Gas), Heavy & Medium French Mortar Ammn to Convent Dump. SH.F. 51.26.NW. H.31.c.4.9. all Lorries were all lorries satisfactorily after an arduous journey, being frequently under the enemy's Shell Fire. On the Return journey the 3rd Party belonging to B Echelon suffered casualties as follows: No 141B. Dr C. CREFTS KILLED, No 68503. Dr T. HUGHES, No 43724 Dr R. ALDOUS wounded & 4 horses killed, 5 wounded (since destroyed).	
	30.5.17	—	1 N.Co 19 wer. Dr. 6 277th AFA R to for Ammunition Fatigue. lowing D.A.C. very short-handed.	
	31.5.17	—	Big Convoy of Heavy French Mortar Ammn unable to be delivered at Convent Dump owing to Gas Shell Barrage. DAC proceed: Lightening of Ammunition on several occasions when working on High Pressure.	

1st June 1917 J.R. Hunt Lt. Col R.A.
Commanding 41 DACRFA

Army Form C. 2118

WAR DIARY
or
~~INTELLIGENCE~~ SUMMARY
(Erase heading not required.)

41st D.A.C. R.F.A.

WM/3

Place	Date	Hour	Summary of Events and Information	Remarks and references to Appendices
Same Place	1/6/17	—	Supplying Ammunition in Wagons & on Pack Animals Nightly to New Gun Positions. ST ELOI Sector until 6/6/17. The Day previous to attack working at high Pressure.	
"	2/6/17	—	Divisional HORSE SHOW. Unit awarded 3 Firsts + 2 Highly Commended.	
"	3/6/17	—	1 Horse Wounded.	
"	5/6/17	—	LT J.B. Ridge, Lt J.G. Tott + 2nd Lt J.H. Millar all badly gassed. L/Bdr Miller evacuated. Returned to Duty + Lt Tott was awarded G. England. L/36400 Dr M. King, L/9116 Dr J.J. Smith, L/47209 St J. Grove, L/37351 Dr Milliam, 55539 D/F Green wounded. 1 Horse Killed 4 Animals Wounded. Fatigue men Returned from Digging in Front Line.	
"	7/6/17	—	No 17330 Cpl T. McNulty, wounded. No 43784 D.W. Goddard awarded the Military Medal for Gallantry on 30/31 May 17	
"	11/6/17 to 24/6/17	—	On an average 36 Wagon Teams + Gunner employee in Salvage work in the Divisional Area. 7th Army Battalion, 4th Son Battery + 7.T.M. Ammunition returned to the Divisional Dump. Enemy T.M. Retrieved + carted to Ordnance Depot.	
"	12/6/17	—	No L 1329 Gr H.E. Slater was highly complimented by G.O.C.R.A. 41 Division for gallant behaviour, whilst ½p of Wagon + Teams at the DAMMSTRASSE under very Heavy shell Fire.	
"	13/6/17	—	Handed over Ammt Dump. G.24.d. to II Corps. Took over New Site Defaulters Ammt Dump at SLT. 28. S.W. N.W. c. 5. 3. 30 Gunners attached to 189 B.G. for work at the Guns.	
"	15/6/17	—	Handed over the Ammn Dump G. 29. C. to 30th DIVISION.	
"	25/6/17	—	Intermittent Shelling of vicinity of RENING HELST by enemy Long Range Guns. Continued daily, until Tl 24.6.17 when owing to the great danger of the HQ D.A.C. Horse Lines Lr. the H.R. were moved to M. 6. B. 6. B.	
SLT 28 SW M. 6. B. 6. B.	22nd 26/6/17	—	No. 14539 Gunner A. ROZEE Engineer accidentally wounded. Enabling Shell.	

A.R. Hurst. L. Col R.F.A.
Commanding 41 D.A.C. R.F.A.

30/6/17

WAR DIARY or INTELLIGENCE SUMMARY

Army Form C. 2118

41st D.A.C. R.F.A.

1st Sheet

No. C./4

Place	Date	Hour	Summary of Events and Information	Remarks and references to Appendices
M.6. t. 6.8.	5.7.17	—	The whole of the DAC moved in to Rest Bivus in the GODNAERSVELDE AREA Sh. 27 Q.24.a & c.	
Q.24.a	11.7.17	—	The Ammn Dump was handed over to 47th Dn. 27 Whitelaw H/O Gunner proceeded up the Line attached to 189 Army S.A.A. for gun pit digging & other work.	
Q.24.a	12.7.17	—	No. L 1508. Dr G. Pope DIED "OEDEMA of LUNGS".	
	18.7.17	—	B Echelon moved back to myring. Killer M.2.a.2.1. 2nd wagon teams were lent to Divisional Reps. from the fatigue & remained away until the 24.7.17.	
			27 (Temp/Lt) T.S.B. Ridge promoted a/capt. whilst commanding a Section took over Command of B Ech.	
	19.7.17	—	Football Team Reached Final Tie in Divisional Tournament – prize despite by R.A.M.C. 4 29 vs G.1.	
	20.7.17	—	Lt Under +12 others from B Ech to 7 Labour Bn. R.E. for Road Mending Fatigues.	
	22.7.17	—	H.Q. D.A.C. moved up to join A.mm Bn. Park B.H.26 SW N.4.c.4.3. 1 No.1 Sec. Cn. M.12.6.2.4. The Dump was taken over from 47 D.A.C. unit 247 O.K. Jones He also in Reserve Dump at N.7.d.0.9i. (LA CLYTTE).	
N.4.C. 4.3.			6 Unites +3 Drs temporarily exchanged with For.6 H.D. Horses +07 the Mules being Required to pull trucks on DECAUVILLE Railway for C.H.A.	
			No. 1555 Dr DYER MA } B. Ech.	
			43701 " THURLOW HC } Wounded	
	23.7.17	—	Some Casualties occurred amongst the Party of Wagons (24) Lent to Divisional RE. 1297 " O'CONNOR M.T.	
			2 Unites Killed + 6 Unites Wounded.	
	25.7.17	—	A/Corp/ 47 D.A.C. in Salvage Work. Loading wagons + Teams & then to cart collects & the Lines to.	
			No. 174923 Br SEALEY J + 1 Horse wounded. (No/Sec) whilst on the Fatigue.	
	25.7.17	—	No. 2 Sec moved up from Rest to S.L.S.S.W. M.6.a.3.5.	
			Since Returning to the Front Line. MO collection have been stampeded by High Bursting by Aeroplane & gas shells.	
			The following Extract from R.O. 2nd Army. 87. 10/7/17.	
			GALLANT CONDUCT	92a
			The Army Commander wishes to express his appreciation of the Gallant conduct of No. 46375 Bombardier F. CULSHAW. B. Ech. 41 DAC under the following circumstances.—	
			"On 16th June 1917 an observation balloon fell in flames on Bar. Culshaw Rushed into the Burning Barn right gear Alignments through the Roof of the Barn. Door when he was overcome by smoke realised by help, carried the others to the Barn Door when he was overcome by smoke realised by help, after recovering over the observer, he again entered the Bdr in search of something belonging to the observer, some of which he found. He stumbled over the N.C.O. i/c of the Car, and he made all the entry of the Barn actually he brought the Conduct Aboard the N.C.O. h accordance with K.R. para. 1919 (XIV)."	

31/7/17

H.F. Urquhart
Lt. Col. L.R.F.A.
COMMANDING 41 D.A.C. R.F.A.

WAR DIARY or INTELLIGENCE SUMMARY

Army Form C. 2118

WD/15

41st D.A.C. R.F.A.

Place	Date	Hour	Summary of Events and Information	Remarks and references to Appendices
N.4.C.5.3.	2/8/17		8 G.S. Wagons & 13 Teams to 128 H.B. R.G.A. to supply Ammn. to Siege Guns & 6" Hows. owing to the Rly. being inoperative for bringing up guns. Horses wounded in N.T.R. by Bomb splinters.	
	13.8.17		No 1 Sec. owing to state of ground in Horse lines moved to new Billet M.6.d.5.6.	
	14.8.17		No 2 Sec. moved into White rotation or M.6.a central CHIPPEWA CAMP.	
	15.8.17		No.210119 Dr. A. FARRER + 93119 Dr. T. HARBIRD wounded by Bomb splinters.	
	19/20.8.17		Salvage Partie taken over from 49th D.A.C. R.F.A.	
	21.8.17			
	23.8.17		4 Horses 18 Echelon wounded whilst carrying T.M. Ammunition.	
			Wagons, Teams + Personnel have to R.E. for Road Repair work. Ammunition Supply practically nightly for T.M's. Wagons Teams + Personnel daily carrying Salvage + Ammn from Front Line to A.R.P. receiving Batteries. H.Q.+ 4 Echelon have been nightly harassed by enemy aeroplanes dropping Bombs around the locality of Camps.	

31/8/17

R. Hurst Lt. Col. R.F.A.
Commanding 41 D.A.C. R.F.A.

Army Form C. 2118

WAR DIARY
INTELLIGENCE SUMMARY
(Erase heading not required.)

4th DACPRA

Vol 16

Place	Date	Hour	Summary of Events and Information	Remarks and references to Appendices
N.4.c.4.3	1/9/17	—	Dump handed over to 39th Division. H.Q. x A. Echelon moved on to R. 5.a. 27. R.5.a.5.6.	
R.5.a.5.6	3/9/17	—	Lt. J. Cross R.F.A. killed by Enemy Aircraft.	
	4/9/17	—	B Echelon. 2 Horses 3 mules wounded by Bombs in Camp.	
	6/9/17	—	2 Officers 34 O.R. fatigue digging gun positions.	
	9/9/17	—	H.Q. x No 1 x 2 Sec. moved up into the Forward Area in R. 28 SW. N.3.6.7.5.	
N.3.6.7.5	10/9/17	—	Took over Dump. N.A.C.K.J. again from 39th Division.	
	12/9/17	—	No 212265 Dr. Gardner F. 17706 & Wilson H. 46005 Dr. Hammond F. 80053 Dr. Gardiner F.H. L/277 Dr. Gear F.E.	
	18/9/17	—	mortally wounded. 1 O.R. attached on Front Line digging gun positions.	
	19/9/17	—	Since wounded.	
		—	No. L/1563 G. Williams S. 19652 R. McDonald D. wounded.	
	22/9/17	—	3 Horses killed & 4 wounded. Nos. Lee by Bombs in Camp. No. 45007 A. Hopkins J.P. No. 66153 R. Ranstone S.	
		—	Nos. Lee wounded by bombs. No. 733 S/E.P. Stock stock whilst on Ammn. Salvage. No. 127,214 R. Hall T.	
		—	wounded whilst digging in the Front Line.	
	23/9/17	—	No 43455 G. Tanner F.C. wounded whilst on fatigue in Front Line.	
	27/9/17	—	No. 113069 G. Francis D.T. Killed & L/36833 Dr. Hood C.F. wounded by bombs. also 1 Horse & 3 mules killed. 5	
		—	Horses & 12 mules wounded.	
	29/9/17	—	2 mules killed while shifting Ammn.	
	30/9/17	—	No. 124,758 R. Dowran L/527 Dr. Harber E. L/47181 M. Adams H. killed & 94067 BSM Morris F. L/7094 Dr. Monteith	
		—	1301 Dr. Murphy J. 146408 Dr. Greenhaugh W.J. 1446964 & Samuels B. wounded by Bombs in the Camp.	

30/9/17

Delivering Ammunition under very trying conditions, the behaviour of all Ranks is beyond praise.
Enemy Aircraft had bombed this unit practically every night during the past month, causing much inconvenience.
All Gunners were sent up the Line to relieve the detachments of 187th Bde. for 96 hours on the 27th June.

Geo. Crookshank Capt. R.F.A.
Commanding 4th DACRA

WAR DIARY
INTELLIGENCE SUMMARY
(Erase heading not required.)

Army Form C. 2118

Vol / 17
4 / O.D.A.C. R.F.A.

Place	Date	Hour	Summary of Events and Information	Remarks and references to Appendices
Jp 3. 6. 7. 5.	1.10.17	—	92819 L Hordler F. Wounded & 2 Horses Killed No 1 Sec. 2 Horses wounded by Enemy Shell Fire No 2 Sec.	
	2.10.17	—	47139 Dr Willier 2 Sec. wounded by Bomb. 1 Horse wounded enemy Shell Fire.	
	3.10.17	—	No L47224 Dr Gifford & L1858 Dr Alrich H. L43715 Dr Bennett F No 2 Sec. wounded delivering Ammunition Up 152 Pte L. Davies M. 3 Sec. Shell Shock. No 1 Sec. 2 Horses Killed, No 2 Sec 1 Mule Killed. 2 Wounded. 1 Horse wounded. No 3 Sec. 2 Mules Killed.	
	7.10.17	—	DAC went by hard Route to WAEMERS — CAPPEL Sh. HAZEBROUCK 5A F.3.	
	8.10.17	—	Continued march to ST POL. SH. DUNKERQUE 1 A E.3. bivouac in Camp near FORT MARDICK	
X.7. C E.7.	14.10.17	—	Marched from ST. POL to COXYDE — BAINS SH 11 S.E. X.7. C.8.7. No 1 Sec. X.7.a.2.6. No 2 Sec. X7. a.3.4. No 3 W. 17. a.w. 7. Took over from A.R.P. LANCASTER. X.3.C.3.4. & STANWAY R.29.C Central.	
	17.10.17	—	No 226476 Dr Murra A. No 1 Sec wounded 1 Mule wounded & Killed. No 2 Sec moved X.7. Central.	
	23.10.17	—	No 46450 Dr Blake Q. B. Ect wounded. No 150385 Dr Sulloch N A. & L45035 Dr Perry F. W. No 2 Sec both Killed in Bivouac. It being Surrounded by Enemy Shells.	
	24.10.17	—	No 37165 Dr Jones N.E. Died of wounds. 45576 Dr Sheard P. Shell Shock No 1 Sec. 4 6 Mules Killed by Hostile Fire.	
	25.10.17	—	No 2 Sec moved owing to Shell Fire to X 2 d Central.	
D. 22.	29.10.17	—	Column moved to GHYVELDE. Sh. DUNKERQUE. Sh. DUNKERQUE 1 A 6.3. Sh 19 D. 22.	

Early in the month the whole of the energy of the DAC was centred on supplying 190th & 8th R.F.A with Ammunition. A very difficult feat, but performed extremely well in vex. terrifying & adverse conditions.

On leaving the DICKEBUSCH area the Unit experienced a very trying march on the 1st day. Cold winds having to travel the whole day.

On arriving Coxyde Area No 1 Sec. was detailed to provide Horse & Vehicle for the 158th Bgde This Brigade had no Animal what-so-ever.

Salvage work Supply of Horses Vehicles to S.M. T.D. for Fatigues & forgoing to Batteries for carting RE material up the line carried on during the Coxyde Period.

The enemy constantly bombed & shelled the Unit throughout, causing many casualties among both Men & Horses, Trying sectors to move position. Behaviour of all Ranks during this trying work was excellent.

3/10/19

A.R.Keevil, Lt. Col. R.A
Commanding 4/1 D.A.C. R.F.A

www.ingramcontent.com/pod-product-compliance
Lightning Source LLC
Chambersburg PA
CBHW081251170426
43191CB00037B/2119